STORIES AND RHYMES

EDITOR

Sally Gray

ASSISTANT EDITOR

Lesley Sudlow

ILLUSTRATOR

Ann Kronheimer

COVER

Lynne Joesbury

SERIES DESIGNER

Sarah Rock

DESIGNER

Heather C Sanneh

AUTHORS

Linda Mort and Janet Morris

Published by Scholastic Ltd,
Villiers House, Clarendon Avenue,
Leamington Spa, Warwickshire CV32 5PR

© 2000 Scholastic Ltd Text © 2000 Linda Mort and Janet Morris
1 2 3 4 5 6 7 8 9   0 1 2 3 4 5 6 7 8 9

British Library Cataloguing-in-Publication Data
A catalogue record for this book is available from the British Library.

ISBN 0-439-01744-0

The publishers gratefully acknowledge permission to reproduce the following copyright material:
'When All The Cows Were Sleeping' Words by Mollie Russell-Smith © EMI Mills Ltd
Worldwide print rights controlled by Warner Bros Publictions Inc, USA/IMP Ltd
Reproduced by permission of IMP Ltd

CONTENTS

Using themes

Gareth, aged four, at tea-time:

'Dad, I've not eaten all my baked beans. Can we plant them?'

'Why?'

'So they'll grow into a baked beanstalk – I want to climb up it!'

Very young children learn by assimilating information from an infinite variety of sources which have no subject boundaries. Children at this stage in their lives are constantly defining and redefining their understanding of the world around them. In order to do this effectively, they need to be provided with experiences that appeal to their imagination and innate need for physical and sensory exploration. A further prerequisite for successful learning is ample opportunity for talking with interested adults.

A thematic approach in the early years is ideally suited to the eclectic way that very young children learn. From an adult perspective, such an approach enables us to plan for the provision of essential learning opportunities in a stimulating and motivating way based on first-hand experiences.

Stories, songs and rhymes have always held a unique place in young children's learning. From the first gentle hand-tickling of rhymes such as 'Round and Round the Garden', a tiny baby is involved in active communication with another person in a very enjoyable way. Throughout the early years, the enormous variety of nursery rhymes, action and counting rhymes and songs offer children ways to develop their social skills, as they learn to take turns and interact with one another. Some rhymes, like stories, give children opportunities to overcome worries and fears and to 'be' another person in their imagination. Stories and rhymes, as well as offering a wealth of opportunities to develop children's language and literacy skills, also provide a basis for stimulating cross-curricular links.

How to use this book

The book is divided into four chapters, the first concentrating on traditional stories, the second on fairy-tales, the third on nursery rhymes, and the last chapter on action and counting rhymes. For each story or rhyme within the chapters, there are three activities – a total of 18 activities per chapter. The activities in this book are clearly linked with QCA's Early Learning Goals and cover all the six areas of learning. There is a photocopiable sheet for each activity, which is designed as an 'end product'. At the beginning of each chapter, the teachers' notes explain each activity and how to maximize the potential of the photocopiable sheets. Within each activity, there is a description of the learning objective, a recommended group size and description of what to do, including suggestions for simplifying and extending the activity for younger or older children.

Using the photocopiable sheets

The photocopiable sheets are designed to be used at the end of each activity. It is very important that before being given the sheets, the children are given plenty of opportunity to explore the rhyme or story as actively as possible using a wide range of readily available resources. For example, before completing the photocopiable sheets based on 'When All the Cows Were Sleeping', let the children dress up as scarecrows. Alternatively, make one together using an upturned mop standing in a bucketful of damp sand.

For some of the activities, it is suggested that in addition to making A4-sized copies of the sheet for the children, an enlarged A3-sized version is also made, for use on a display easel. The activity notes give suggestions for using the enlarged sheets as part of the active learning process with the group, before the children tackle their individual sheets. You may also like to laminate some of the sheets for group games or displays.

Links with home

Encourage the children to take some of their photocopiable sheets home to talk about with their families. Keep others in the children's files to record progress and for assessment purposes. An enlarged sheet can form the basis of an interactive, three-dimensional display, which the children can talk about with the adults who bring them to, or collect them from, nursery or school. Other photocopiable sheets such as 'Wishes' (page 41) or 'My dream' (page 91), can be made into little books for the children to share with their families.

Encourage the children to bring in books and artefacts relevant to the stories and rhymes that you are focusing on. Make a display of different books on the same theme for the children to talk about similarities and differences. Invite parents to come in and tell their own favourite stories and rhymes to the class.

Old Mother Hubbard

Old Mother Hubbard
Went to the cupboard,
To fetch her poor dog a bone;
But when she got there,
The cupboard was bare
And so the poor dog had none.

Jack and Jill

Jack and Jill went up the hill
To fetch a pail of water;
Jack fell down and broke his crown,
And Jill came tumbling after.

Up Jack got, and home did trot,
As fast as he could caper;
He went to bed to mend his head
With vinegar and brown paper.

Mary, Mary, Quite Contrary

Mary, Mary, quite contrary,
How does your garden grow?
With silver bells and cockle shells,
And pretty maids all in a row.

Humpty Dumpty

Humpty Dumpty sat on a wall,
Humpty Dumpty had a great fall;
All the King's horses and all the King's men
Couldn't put Humpty together again.

Hey Diddle, Diddle,

Hey diddle, diddle,
The cat and fiddle,
The cow jumped over the moon;
The little dog laughed
To see such fun,
And the dish ran away with the spoon.

Hickory, Dickory, Dock

Hickory, dickory, dock,
The mouse ran up the clock.
The clock struck One,
The mouse ran down,
Hickory, dickory, dock!

Here We Go Round the Mulberry Bush

Here we go round the Mulberry Bush,
The Mulberry Bush, the Mulberry Bush,
Here we go round the Mulberry Bush
On a cold and frosty morning.

Miss Polly Had a Dolly

Miss Polly had a dolly who was sick, sick, sick.
So she called for the doctor to be quick, quick, quick;
The doctor came with his bag and his hat,
And he knocked on the door with a rat-a-tat-tat.
He looked at the dolly, and he shook his head,
And he said, 'Miss Polly, put her straight to bed'.
He wrote on a paper for a pill, pill, pill,
'That will make her better, yes it will, will, will'.

When All the Cows Were Sleeping

When all the cows were sleeping, and the sun had gone to bed,
Up jumped the scarecrow, and this is what he said:
'I'm a dingle-dangle scarecrow with a flippy, floppy hat.
I can shake my hands like this, and shake my feet like that!'

When all the hens were roosting, and the moon behind a cloud,
Up jumped the scarecrow, and shouted very loud:
'I'm a dingle-dangle scarecrow...'.

When the dogs were in the kennel, and the doves were in the loft,
Up jumped the scarecrow, and whispered very soft:
'I'm a dingle-dangle scarecrow...'.

© M Russell-Smith and G Russell-Smith

Five Currant Buns

Five currant buns in a baker's shop,
Round and fat with sugar on the top.
Along came a boy with a penny one day,
Bought a currant bun and took it away.

Four currant buns...

There Were Ten in the Bed

There were ten in the bed,
And the little one said,
'Roll over! Roll over!'
So they all rolled over
And one fell out.

There were nine in the bed...

There was one in the bed,
And the little one said,
'Good-night, good-night'.

One, Two, Buckle My Shoe

One, two, buckle my shoe,
Three, four, knock at the door.
Five, six, pick up sticks,
Seven, eight, lay them straight.
Nine, ten, a big fat hen,
Eleven, twelve, dig and delve.
Thirteen, fourteen, maids a-courting,
Fifteen, sixteen, maids in the kitchen.
Seventeen, eighteen, maids in waiting,
Nineteen, twenty, my plate's empty.

TRADITIONAL STORIES

PAGE 13
HOW MUCH GRASS?

Learning objective
To understand the terms 'a little', 'more' and 'most'. (Mathematical Development)

Group size
Up to four children.

(Story – 'The Three Billy Goats Gruff'.) Copy the photocopiable sheet for each child. Cut some grass with large scissors and store in an airtight container. Ask the children to point to the 'little', 'medium-sized' and 'big' goat. Who would eat a 'little', 'more' and the 'most' grass? Ask each child to stick the appropriate amount of real grass by each goat. (Make sure that none of the children have allergies to grass.) Draw an appropriately-sized rectangle by each goat for younger children and ask them to fill each one with grass.

PAGE 14
HOOFPRINTS!

Learning objective
To move imaginatively. (Physical Development)

Group size
Three children.

(Story – 'The Three Billy Goats Gruff'.) Make three enlarged copies of the photocopiable sheet, cut out the hoofprints and stick them onto individual sheets of A5 card. Chalk two lines on the floor to represent the bridge. Arrange three sets of prints for one of the goats along the bridge. Which goat do they belong to? Invite one of the children to move across the bridge on all fours, with small, medium or

large footsteps as appropriate. Tell younger children who the prints belong to. Extend the activity for older children by inviting them to make prints for different animals.

PAGE 15
TRIP, TRAP!

Learning objective
To play loud, medium and quiet drumbeats. (Creative Development)

Group size
Seven children.

(Story – 'The Three Billy Goats Gruff'.) Make three copies of the photocopiable sheet and stick each one on the lid of an empty rectangular biscuit tin. Choose four children to be the troll and goats, and three children to be the 'drummers'. Ask the goats to take it in turns to 'trip, trap' across the bridge. Each goat should be accompanied by a drummer who uses a drumstick to tap (at the appropriate sound level) on top of the drumstick pictures on the tin. Let younger children tap with their hands and suggest that older children vary their 'speed' from quick (smallest goat) to slow (biggest goat).

PAGE 16
YES, OF COURSE!

Learning objective
To act out an alternative version of a familiar tale. (Personal, Social and Emotional Development)

Group size
Four children.

(Story – 'The Little Red Hen'.) Remind the children of the story and explain that together you are going to act out a different version where the animals help the hen. Act out the story with the children saying, 'Yes, of course!' each time. Give one copy of the photocopiable sheet to each child and help them to cut out the speech bubbles. Let each child stick the bubbles in the correct places. For younger children, number each bubble and space for them to match. Enlarge the sheet for older children and blank out the words in the speech bubbles. Encourage them to use emergent writing to fill the bubbles.

PAGE 17
WHO ARE YOU?

Learning objective
To read and spell simple three letter words. (Language and Literacy)

Group size
Three children.

(Story – 'The Little Red Hen'.) Make three copies of the photocopiable sheet and cut out the words. Give each child a sheet and encourage them to work out the words for themselves. Give each child their three cut out word cards and ask them to match the words to the words and pictures on their sheet. Encourage older children to cut up the words into individual letters and ask them to scramble them up and reassemble them.

PAGE 18
ROUND AND ROUND

Learning objective
To make a moving windmill picture. (Knowledge and Understanding of the World)

Group size
Up to four children.

(Story – 'The Little Red Hen'.) Provide each child with a copy of the photocopiable sheet. Cut along the line and help each child to cut out the sails and attach them to the windmill with a split pin. Help them to cut out the characters and let them arrange and stick them onto the picture. Encourage the children to draw extra details such as other characters and clouds. Enlarge the photocopiable sheet for younger children. Let older children stick their picture onto a cereal box and cut an opening door in the windmill to make a 3-D scene. Mount the characters onto card and make into puppets using clean lolly sticks.

PAGE 19
PASS IT ON!

Learning objective
To explore the idea of working together. (Personal, Social and Emotional Development)

Group size
Up to four children.

(Story – 'The Enormous Turnip'.) Talk about how people can pass objects to each other by standing 'side by side'. Let the children practise this together. Remind the children of the story and explain that as the turnip was too heavy for one person, the old man cut it into pieces which he passed along the 'chain'. Provide each child with a photocopiable sheet copied onto thin card. Cut out the strip of characters for the children. Ask them to draw in the rest of the details of the characters and to fold the strip into a concertina. Let older children cut out the figures to make a 'chain'.

PAGE 20
IN A LINE

(Story – 'The Enormous Turnip'.) Make a copy of the photocopiable sheet for each child plus one spare. Stick all the sheets onto card. Help the children to cut out and fold the characters as indicated. An adult should cut the slits in the children's sheets using a craft knife. Stick each character from the spare sheet onto pieces of larger card and add ribbon, so that each child can wear one like a necklace. Remind the children of the sequence of the story and show them how to mime pulling up the 'turnip' as a team. Now ask the children to mix up their folded card characters and then insert them in the slits so that they stand up in the correct order, using the words, 'first, second' and so on. Put the characters in order for younger children.

Learning objective
To understand the terms 'first', 'second' and so on. (Mathematical Development)

Group size
Seven children.

PAGE 21
SOUP BOWL

(Story – 'The Enormous Turnip'.) Copy the photocopiable sheet for each child and ask them to use a pencil to write the initial letters of their name in a repeating pattern between the lines round the bowl. (Some children will need an adult to write the letters faintly, or a dot for the starting point). Place a tray in the centre of the table with containers of different coloured dried peas, beans, lentils and so on. Ask each child to choose two different kinds to stick onto their letters using glue sticks. Use the initial letters of first names only for younger children.

Learning objective
To decorate a soup bowl with initials. (Creative Development)

Group size
Up to five children.

PAGE 22
WHO SAID THAT?

(Story – 'The Three Little Pigs'.) Copy the photocopiable sheet for each child, cut along the slits and cut out the two strips. Remind the children of the story and encourage them to tell you about the materials that the three pigs chose to build their houses with. Ask each child to thread the strips through the slots, and pull them along to match the speech bubbles to each of the characters in turn. Give younger children picture clues by drawing the relevant objects in the bubbles.

PAGE 23
HOUSE OF BRICKS

(Story – 'The Three Little Pigs'.) Take the children to see a brick wall. Draw their attention to the way bricks are arranged to overlap. Explain that this makes a wall good and strong. Let the children practise building their own walls with construction kits. Can they copy a brick wall pattern? Copy the photocopiable sheet for each child, cut out the bricks and ask them to glue the bricks in the same pattern as the brick wall. Draw the vertical 'cement' lines to help younger children to place their bricks. Let older children pool their bricks, throw a dice in turn and take the appropriate number of bricks from the 'kitty' until a winner completes their house.

PAGE 24
HEAVY LOADS

(Story – 'The Three Little Pigs'.) Remind the children of the materials that the three pigs used to build their houses. Which one was the lightest? Which was the heaviest? Ask each child to choose a 'load' to carry, and to mime carrying it, indicating through movements and gestures which load is being carried – the 'light' straw, the 'heavier' wood or the 'heaviest' bricks. Copy the photocopiable sheet for each child and let them draw in the correct load for each pig. Let older children use collage materials to represent the different loads.

PAGE 25
DOES IT MATTER?

(Story – 'The Town Mouse and the Country Mouse'.) Have a discussion with the children about how people behave towards each other. Explain that the way people behave is much more important than the things that they own. Make a copy of the photocopiable sheet for each child and talk about it together. Ask them to draw one more picture in each set and to circle the words, 'yes' or 'no', accordingly. Let younger children simply circle 'yes' or 'no' and suggest that older children make a group book entitled 'Does it matter?'.

PAGE 26
I SPY!

(Story – 'The Town Mouse and the Country Mouse'.) Copy the photocopiable sheet for each child and fold in half vertically, so that only one side of the sheet is visible at a time. Play a game of 'I Spy' using the pictures. Ask the children to find the item and then draw a line between it and its initial letter below. Simplify the game for younger children by making the letter sound then asking them to choose the correct match from a choice of two. Suggest that older children write over the letters as they match each one.

TOWN OR COUNTRY?

(Story – 'The Town Mouse and the Country Mouse'.) Enlarge and copy the photocopiable sheet for each child. Ask the children to cut out the items and stick them to the appropriate town or country landscape. Cut out the items for younger children. Copy or mount the sheet onto thin card for older children and encourage them to cut out the items and stick each one onto a small box to create interesting 3-D landscape pictures.

ALMOST NEW SHOES

(Story – 'The Elves and the Shoemaker'.) Bring in an old shoe and take it apart to let the children see how it is constructed. Let the children examine the soles and heels of their shoes. Explain that occasionally, some shoes need to have their soles and/or heels repaired, and that shoemakers must choose the correct size and shape of soles and heels, before gluing them onto the old shoes. Give each child a copy of the photocopiable sheet and ask them to draw lines to match the person with the correct shoe, heel and sole. Ask younger children to match the people and shoes only. Open a 'shoe repair' shop for older children. Ask them to draw around their shoes on sugar paper, cut out the shapes, then cut these shapes into 'heels' and 'soles'. Show them how to put a piece of folded sticky tape in the centre of the soles and heels, so that they may stick new shapes on top.

SEW THE SHOES

(Story – 'The Elves and the Shoemaker'.) Give each child a copy of the photocopiable sheet and help them to punch a hole on top of each dot, using a single-hole hole-punch. Provide a blunt tapestry needle and ribbon or wool for each child and help them to sew around the template. Punch the holes for younger children. Use the templates as patterns for felt boots for older children. Punch holes in the felt and work closely with the children to sew them together using blunt needles and wool or ribbon.

MEALTIME

(Story – 'The Elves and the Shoemaker'.) Provide each child with a copy of the photocopiable sheet stuck onto card. Ask each child to decorate and cut out their plate. What sort of food do the children think the elves would like to eat? Ask them to use play dough, Plasticine or salt dough to make some food to go on the elves' plates. Show younger children how to make simple items such as 'peas', 'sausages' and 'pancakes'. Encourage older children to find photographs of food from magazines to cut out and stick onto their plate.

How much grass?

◆ Stick the correct amount of grass next to each goat.

Hoofprints!

◆ Put your hands and feet on these prints and move like a goat!

Trip, trap!

◆ Tap on the drumsticks.

Trip, trap!

Trip, trap!

Trip, trap!

Trip, trap!

Trip, trap!

Trip, trap!

Trip, trap!

Trip, trap!

Trip, trap!

Yes, of course!

◆ Stick the speech bubbles in the correct place.

Will you help me plant my grains of wheat, please?

Woof, woof! Yes, of course!

Will you help me plant my grains of wheat, please?

Eek, eek! Yes, of course!

Will you help me plant my grains of wheat, please?

Meeow, meeow! Yes, of course!

Who are you?

◆ Read and match the words.

dog	rat	cat

Round and round

◆ Cut out the characters and stick on to make a picture of 'The Little Red Hen' story.

Pass it on!

Finish the pictures.

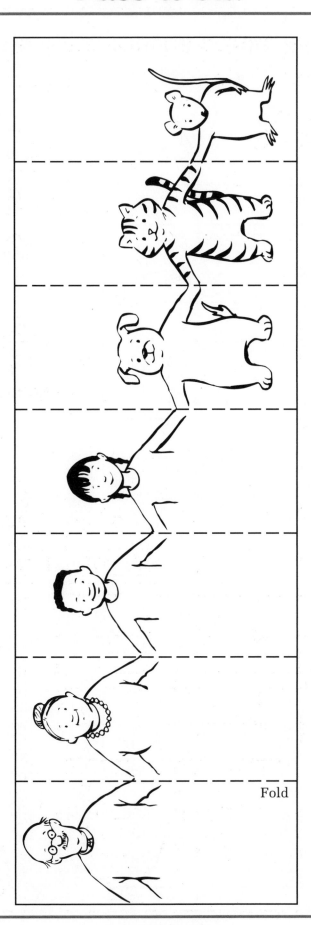

Fold

In a line

◆ Cut out and fold the characters. Put them in a line.

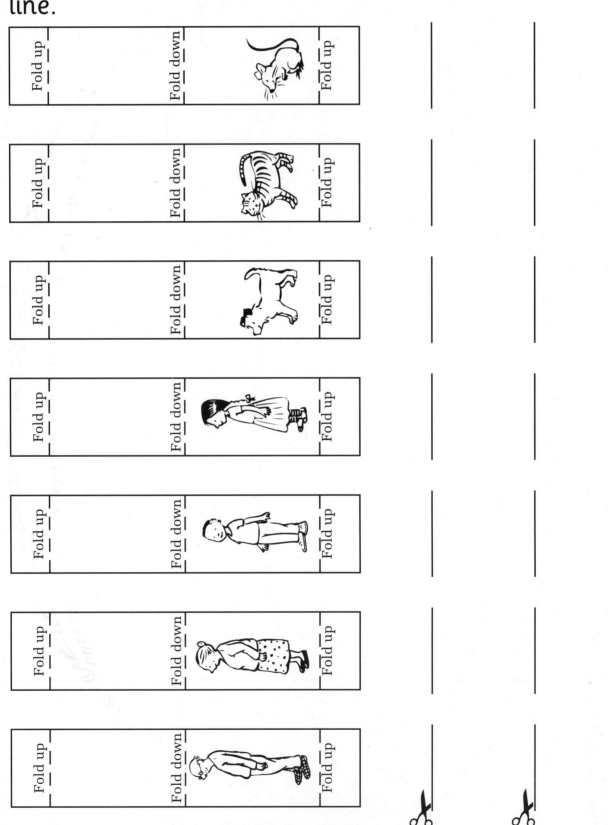

Soup bowl

◆ Write your initials on the soup bowl. Make a pattern.

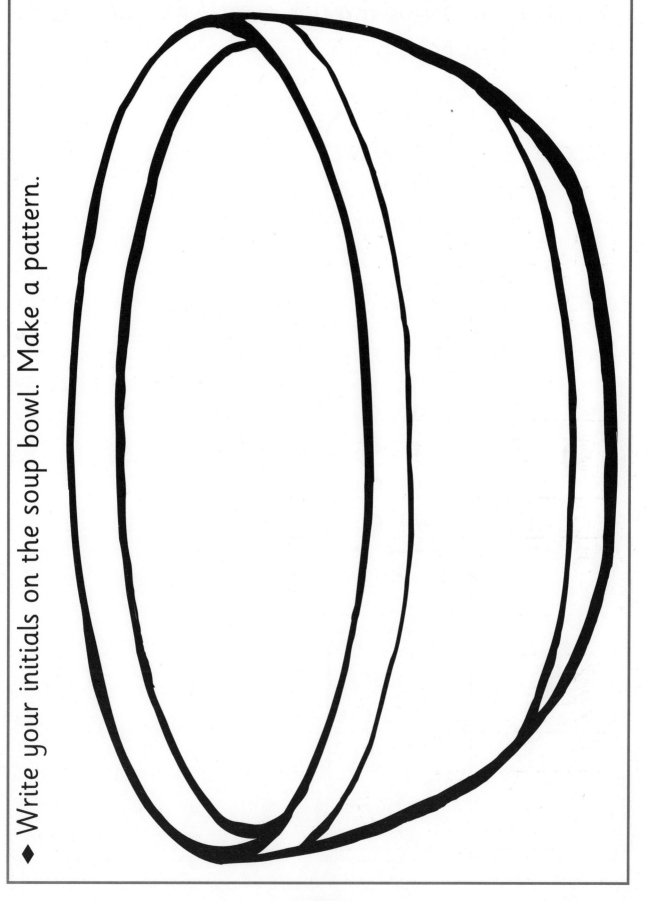

Who said that?

◆ Thread the strips through the slits to make the words match each pig.

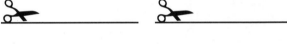

House of bricks

◆ Arrange the bricks on the house.

Heavy loads

◆ Show what each pig is carrying.

 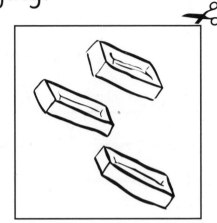

 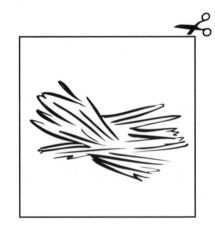

 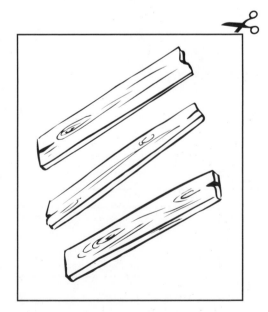

Does it matter?

...if you live in a

 or [ ] ? | yes | no |

...if you have

 or [ ] ? | yes | no |

...if you wear

 or [ ] ? | yes | no |

...if you are caring and sharing

 or [ ] ? | yes | no |

I Spy!

◆ Draw lines to match the objects to their letters.

Country	Town

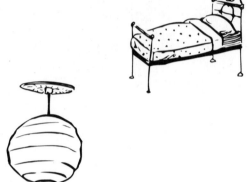

c   **h**   b   b   **t**   b

f   j   l   r

Town or country?

◆ Cut out and stick the pictures in the town or countryside.

Almost new shoes

◆ Draw lines to match the people with the correct shoe, heel and sole.

Sew the shoes

◆ Sew these shoes for the elves.

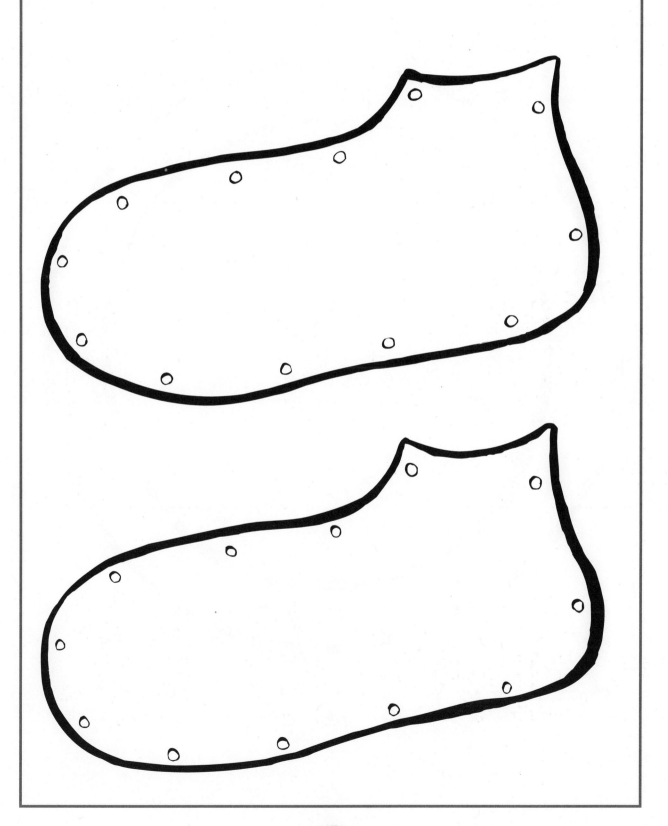

Mealtime

◆ Make some food for the elves to eat.

FAIRY-TALES

PAGE 35
GETTING BIGGER

Learning objective
To order bowls and spoons by size. (Mathematical Development)

Group size
Three children.

(Story – 'Goldilocks and the Three Bears'.) Let the children practise size matching using real teddies, bowls and spoons. Enlarge the photocopiable sheet to A3-size and make a copy for each child. Make the slits in the bears' paws and cut out the bowls and spoons. Mount the spoons onto thin card. Let the children slot the spoons through the bears' paws and stick the right-sized bowl next to each bear. Encourage younger children to stick the spoons instead of using the slits and invite older children to draw an appropriately sized cup in each bear's free hand.

PAGE 36
MEND THAT CHAIR

Learning objective
To assemble a chair from paper. (Knowledge and Understanding of the World)

Group size
Up to four children.

(Story – 'Goldilocks and the Three Bears'.) Make a copy of the photocopiable sheet, mounted onto thin card, for each child. Ask the children to cut out the shape and fold along the dotted lines, using sticky tape to secure the base (see diagram). Cut out the shape for younger children. Provide enlarged sheets for older children to make two larger chairs in the same way, one for Mummy Bear and one for Daddy Bear.

PAGE 37
THE OTHER HALF

Learning objective
To draw missing house details. (Physical Development)

Group size
Up to four children.

(Story – 'Goldilocks and the Three Bears'.) Provide a small plastic mirror and show the children how to use the mirror with the photocopiable sheet to reflect one side of the picture. Give each child a copy of the sheet and ask them to complete the missing half of the house. Draw dotted lines completing the picture for younger children to trace over. Show older children how to draw on top of the printed side using thick wax crayons, fold over the page and press down on the paper with a rolling pin to produce a 'print' on the blank side of the sheet.

PAGE 38
UP AND DOWN

Learning objective
To read a simple book highlighting the words 'up' and 'down'. (Language and Literacy)

Group size
Up to six children.

(Story – 'Jack and the Beanstalk'.) Make two flashcards, one reading 'up' and one reading 'down'. Circle the word 'up' in red, and 'down' in blue. Make a copy of the photocopiable sheet for each child. Cut out the pictures and staple them into booklets for the children. Display the flashcards and read the book with the children. Ask them to circle the word 'up' in red, and 'down' in blue. Help younger children to match the words with the flashcards and ask older children to design a front cover for their booklet.

PAGE 39

CLIMBING JACK

Learning objective
To make a model of climbing Jack. (Knowledge and Understanding of the World)

Group size
Up to three children.

(Story – 'Jack and the Beanstalk'.) Copy the photocopiable sheet onto thin card for each child. Help them to colour the beanstalk and Jack. Now cut out Jack and then cut along all the lines. Place the blank piece of card underneath the beanstalk picture and then stick adhesive tape down the left-hand side to make a stand-up card. Ask each child to punch a hole in the top of their beanstalk. Stick a piece of string onto Jack and thread the string through the hole, securing it to the blank part of the card with adhesive tape (see diagram). When the card is opened, Jack will appear to climb up the beanstalk. Let younger children use sponges to paint the beanstalk. Invite older children to write 'Jack climbed up and up' inside the card, before attaching the string.

PAGE 40

CAN YOU DO THIS?

Learning objective
To mime key events in a familiar story. (Physical Development)

Group size
Up to six children.

(Story – 'Jack and the Beanstalk'.) Make one copy of the photocopiable sheet onto thin card. Use the sheet to remind the children of the key events of the story. Cut up the pictures and put them in a drawstring bag. Ask one child at a time to pick a card and mime the action for the rest of the group to guess. Help younger children to verbalize the action before miming it. Ask older children to say what happened in the story before and after their mime.

PAGE 41

WISHES

Learning objective
To consider a baby's well-being. (Personal, Social and Emotional Development)

Group size
Up to four children.

(Story – 'Sleeping Beauty'.) Copy the photocopiable sheet onto thin card for each child. Invite them to 'dress' the baby by sticking on fabric scraps, lace, ribbon and so on. Ask them to cut along the solid lines and fold the dotted line to make a card. Talk to the children about what kind of child they would like the 'baby' to grow into – happy, giggly, kind, good at making up games and so on. Write each child's wish inside their card and invite them to write over or copy it underneath. Scribe the wishes for younger children. Encourage older children to write their own wish, using their own level of emergent writing.

PAGE 42

BUILD A CASTLE

Learning objective
To identify solid shapes. (Mathematical Development)

Group size
Two children.

(Story – 'Sleeping Beauty'.) Make one A3-sized copy of the photocopiable sheet, and two A4-sized copies. Display the large copy and ask two children to work together to build a palace in the same way. If cones are unavailable, show the children how to make them from circles of card bent round and secured with sticky tape. Give a sheet to each child and ask them to count the number of each type of shape. Show them how to write the number inside the rectangles above each shape. Let the children copy the numbers from those at the bottom of the page. Ask younger children to draw a line from each solid shape to the right number. For older children, cut off the numbers at the bottom of the sheet.

PAGE 43

SOUNDS LIKE...

Learning objective
To create appropriate sound effects to enact the story. (Creative Development)

Group size
Up to six children.

(Story – 'Sleeping Beauty'.) Ask the children to experiment making sounds with the following items: a maraca; a large piece of card shaken to produce a 'thundery' sound; sleigh bells; coconut shells and wood blocks. Remind the children of the Sleeping Beauty story and ask them to consider which sounds suit the different parts of the story. For example, what sounds like the baby princess playing with a rattle or the

prince approaching the castle on horseback. Ask each child to complete the sheet, by drawing lines between the objects and the pictures, as they listen to each sound being played from behind a screen. Let younger children see the sound effects being made and ask older children to complete the sheet from memory.

PAGE 44
HELPERS

Learning objective
To play a game based on co-operative behaviour. (Personal, Social and Emotional Development)

Group size
Six children.

(Story – 'Cinderella'.) Copy the photocopiable sheet for each child. Explain that after Cinderella and the prince got married, the bossy sisters said they were sorry. Cinderella and the prince said they could all live together, if everybody shared the housework. Give each child four white rectangular peel-off labels and ask them to draw Cinderella, the prince and the sisters on the separate labels. Ask each child to stick a different character onto each picture on the sheet to show that person carrying out the task. Discuss each child's sheet and talk about the different jobs that the characters are doing. Let younger children use play people instead of stickers. Challenge older children to design a sheet for sharing tasks in the garden.

PAGE 45
ALPHABET GAME

Learning objective
To match initial sounds with letters. (Language and Literacy)

Group size
Four children.

(Story – 'Cinderella'.) Make four copies of the photocopiable sheet onto card and laminate. Put the following plastic letters in a drawstring bag: b; d; m; i; f; w; p; l; m; p; c; s. Give each child a sheet and eight counters. Let them cover eight pictures of their choice. Pass round the bag for the children to pick a letter. If they can match one of their pictures to the letter sound then they may uncover that picture. The first child to uncover all eight pictures is the winner. Help younger children by giving a descriptive clue each time – for example, 'It begins with 'm' and you clean the floor with it.' Ask older children to cover all their pictures and play variations of the game, such as matching the final sounds of the words.

PAGE 46
WHAT A GOWN!

(Story – 'Cinderella'.) Make a copy of the photocopiable sheet for each child. Ask them to draw over the outline of the dress in felt-tipped pen and to choose two kinds of coloured sticky shapes. Invite the children to cut out small rectangular pieces of doily and stick them in overlapping fashion over the centre panel to represent lace frills. Ask each child to stick one kind of shape over the two side folds, and the other kind of shape on the bodice. Let younger children stick on the shapes randomly. Encourage older children to cut out the dress, stick it on a larger piece of paper and draw Cinderella's face, shoulders, arms, hands and feet.

Learning objective
To decorate Cinderella's gown. (Creative Development)

Group size
Up to five children.

PAGE 47
HELPING OTHERS

(Story – 'Little Red Riding Hood'.) Talk to the children about ways to help old people such as visiting them, shopping, cooking, cleaning, decorating or gardening for them and so on. Ask each child to draw their own face on the sheet, and that of an old person, perhaps one they know. What would they like to do to help the old person? Write it in the speech bubble for them to write over. Scribe the words for younger children and let older children have a try at the writing themselves.

Learning objective
To discuss ways to help old people. (Personal, Social and Emotional Development)

Group size
Up to four children.

PAGE 48
ALL TALK!

(Story – 'Little Red Riding Hood'.) Make one A3-sized copy of the photocopiable sheet and one A4-sized copy per child. Cut out the speech bubbles from the enlarged sheet. Hold up the bubbles with the children and read them. Discuss which character would have said those words. Use Blu-Tack to stick the bubbles next to the characters. Now ask each child to cut out the bubbles on their sheet and stick them accordingly, referring to the enlarged sheet if necessary. For younger children, colour code the bubbles and characters with matching

Learning objective
To read dialogue. (Language and Literacy)

Group size
Up to four children.

children the seven items already made and help them share them equally between the dwarfs. Put less than, or more than seven items of food on a plate for older children and ask whether there are enough, not enough, too few or too many.

PAGE 51
HEIGH HO!

(Story – 'Snow White'.) Enlarge the photocopiable sheet to A3-size, and make one A4-sized copy per child. Say that the dwarfs mined diamonds, emeralds, rubies and sapphires. If possible, let the children examine replica rings. On the enlarged copy, write over the word 'ruby' in red; 'emerald' in green and so on. Colour the rings. Ask the children to help you match the words and rings using lengths of wool attached with Blu-Tack. Read through the sheet, then remove the wool. Help each child to complete their own sheet and colour the rings using glitter, foil, Cellophane and so on. Help younger children by putting an appropriately coloured dot by the words and rings. Ask older children to find out about four more precious stones and to create a similar sheet.

Learning objective
To learn the colours of precious stones.
(Knowledge and Understanding of the World)

Group size
Up to five children.

dots, then read through the speech bubbles, encouraging them to join in. Ask older children to design a similar sheet based on 'Jack and the Beanstalk'.

PAGE 49
SNAP HAPPY!

Learning objective
To use scissors to make a snapping wolf's jaws.
(Physical Development)

Group size
Up to four children.

(Story – 'Little Red Riding Hood'.) For each child, make a copy of the photocopiable sheet and cut out two card rectangles, each 9cm x 2cm. Draw zigzag lines on the rectangles for a length of 7cm. Using an awl, make a hole at the end of the rectangles and put a split pin through the holes. Invite each child to colour and cut out the wolf from the sheet. Ask them to colour the rectangles brown and cut along the zigzag lines. Make a hole on each wolf and help each child to attach the 'jaws'. For younger children, simply draw on the teeth for them to draw over. Let older children use pinking scissors (under supervision) to cut the teeth.

PAGE 50
ONE EACH!

Learning objective
To develop one-to-one correspondence.
(Mathematical Development)

Group size
Up to four children.

(Story – 'Snow White'.) Make a copy of the photocopiable sheet for each child. Talk about the seven dwarfs and count them. What sort of food would the dwarfs like to eat? Each dwarf needs one piece of food. How many pieces of food will they need all together? Let the children make seven food items from play dough or Plasticine and ask them to give each dwarf one item of food. Give younger

PAGE 52
MIRROR, MIRROR

(Story – 'Snow White'.) Talk to the children about the expressions on the faces of Snow White and the queen. Explain that people's expressions can help to tell us what kind of people they are. Let the children practise making different expressions in a mirror. Make a copy of the photocopiable sheet for each child and ask them to draw Snow White's and the queen's reflections on the sheet. Let younger children draw an egg shape, eyes and nose in each mirror. Give them two cut out red gummed paper 'mouths' and show them how to turn a 'smile' upside-down to make a 'frown'. Let the children stick on the mouths. Encourage older children to draw seven more mirror shapes with the reflections of the seven dwarfs.

Learning objective
To draw the queen's and Snow White's reflections in a mirror.
(Creative Development)

Group size
Up to six children.

Getting bigger

◆ Give each bear their bowl and spoon.

Mend that chair

◆ Cut out and make Baby Bear's chair.

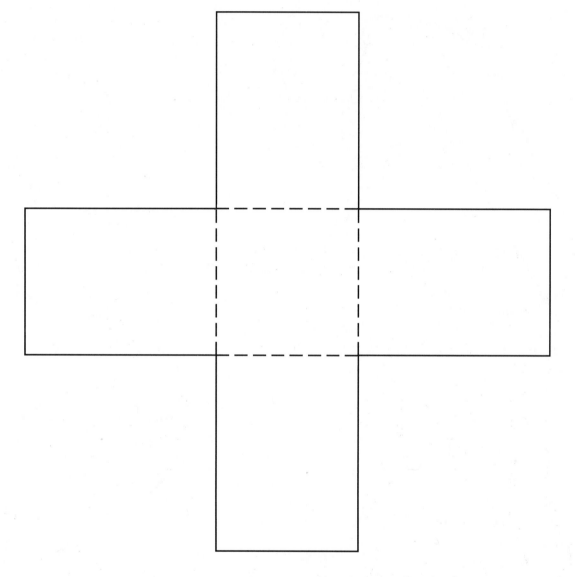

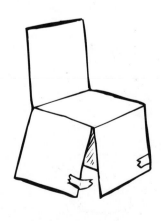

The other half

◆ Draw the other side of the house.

Up and down

◆ Circle the word 'up' in red, and 'down' in blue.

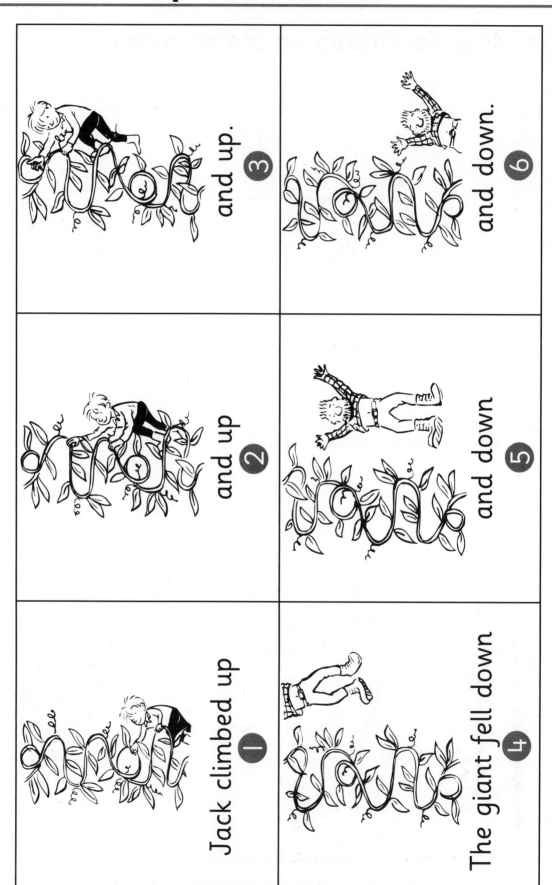

Jack climbed up **1**

and up **2**

and up. **3**

The giant fell down **4**

and down **5**

and down. **6**

Climbing Jack

◆ Make Jack climb up the beanstalk.

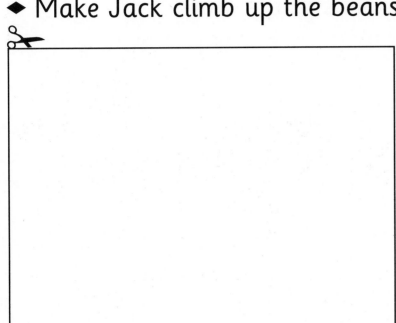

Can you do this?

◆ Mime what happens in the story.

Wishes

◆ Make a card of kind wishes for a baby.

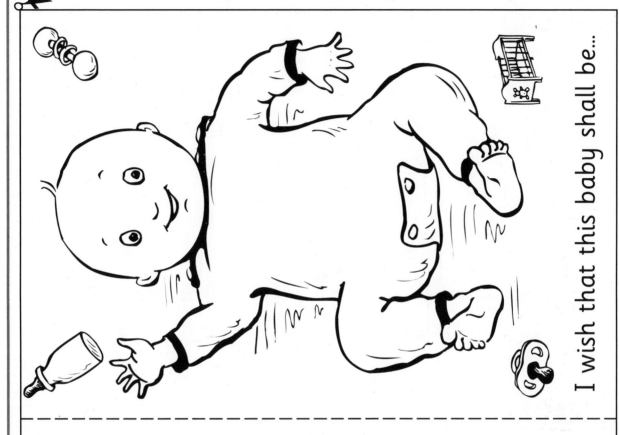

I wish that this baby shall be...

Build a castle

◆ Write down how many of each kind of brick you use.

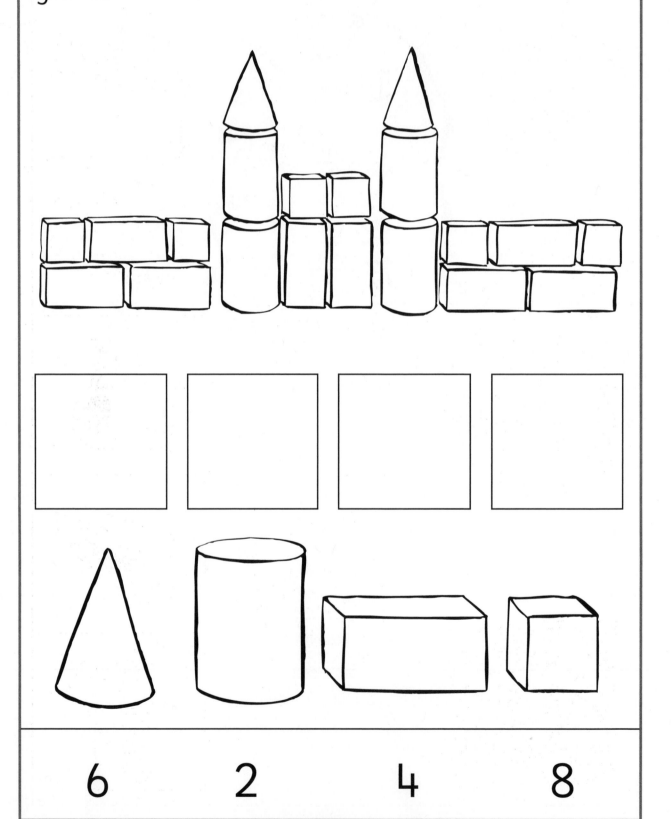

6	2	4	8

Sounds like...

◆ Match each part of the story to a sound.

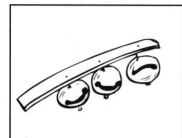

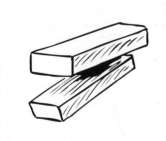

Helpers

◆ Stick one of your labels onto each picture.

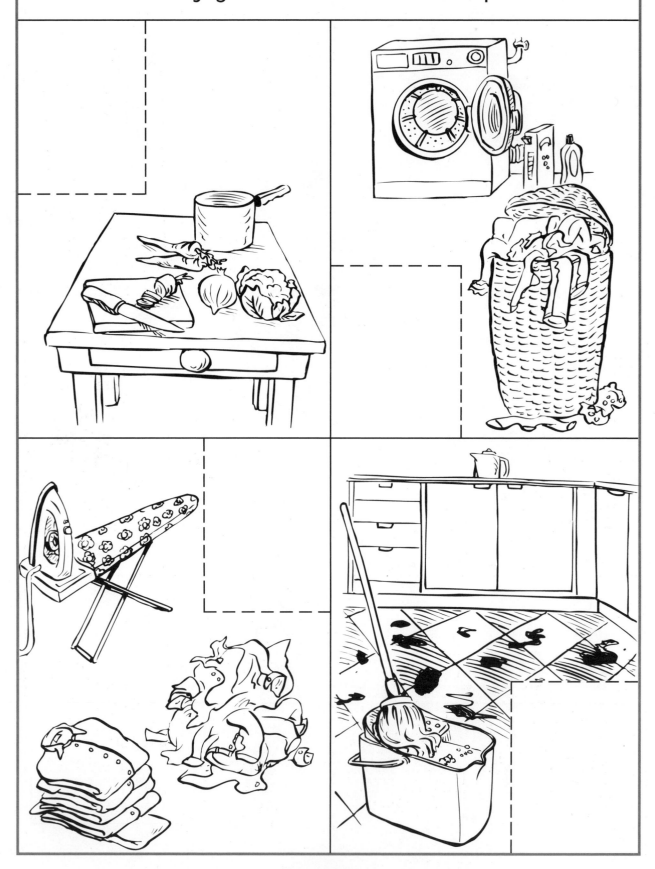

Alphabet game

◆ Listen for the letter sounds.

What a gown!

◆ Decorate the dress for Cinderella.

Helping others

◆ Draw a picture of your face and an old person's face. Write in your speech bubble how you would help them.

How kind!
Thank you very
much!

All talk!

◆ Cut out the speech bubbles and match them to the characters.

What big eyes you have!

Help, help. Let me out of here!

Don't talk to strangers!

All the better to see you with!

Snap happy!

◆ Colour and cut out the wolf. Make some snapping jaws for him.

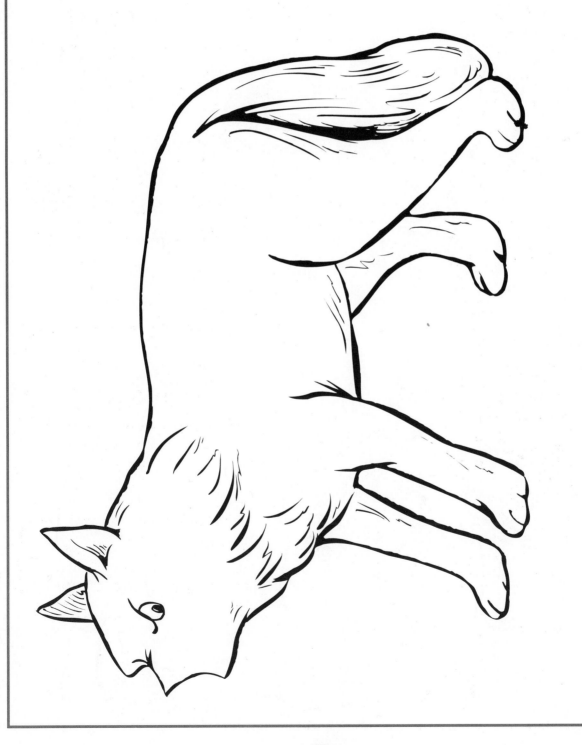

One each!

◆ Give each dwarf one piece of food.

Heigh ho!

◆ Colour the precious stones and match them to their names.

red

emerald

blue

diamond

green

ruby

white

sapphire

Mirror, mirror

◆ Draw the reflections of Snow White and the queen in the mirrors.

NURSERY RHYMES

HAPPY PETS

Learning objective
To think and talk about pets' exercise needs. (Personal, Social and Emotional Development)

Group size
Up to four children.

(Rhyme – 'Old Mother Hubbard'.) Make one A3-size copy of the photocopiable sheet and four A4-size copies. Display the enlarged copy on an easel and talk to the children about how pets need exercise to keep healthy and happy. Point to the pets at the bottom of the sheet and ask the children to say which item would be used by each pet. Draw a line from each item to the appropriate pet. Provide each child with their own copy of the photocopiable sheet and ask them to cut out the pets and stick them next to the relevant pictures. Let younger children simply draw lines between matching pairs. Challenge older children to design a similar sheet showing exercise items used by a baby, child and grown-up.

A FULL CUPBOARD

Learning objective
To make a cupboard from card. (Knowledge and Understanding of the World)

Group size
Up to four children.

(Rhyme – 'Old Mother Hubbard'.) Copy and mount the photocopiable sheet onto card for each child. Ask them to cut along the solid lines and fold inwards along the dotted lines to make Mother Hubbard's cupboard. Say that sometimes, Old Mother Hubbard was lucky enough to have her cupboard full of food. Ask the children to draw some shelves and some special food for Mother Hubbard and her dog. Let the children colour the cupboard doors and draw knobs on them. Cut out the cupboard outline for younger children and challenge older children to design and make a wardrobe full of clothes, in a similar way.

YOUR TURN!

(Rhyme – 'Old Mother Hubbard'.) Copy the photocopiable sheet for each child, and make one enlarged copy. Cut out the pictures from the enlarged copy and display the rhyme on an easel. Read through the rhyme with the children, holding up the relevant pictures and sticking them next to the appropriate verses with Blu-Tack. Choose three children to act out the rhyme. Give them each a picture to act out in turn. Now remove the rhyme from view and ask the children to read through their own sheet and draw a line from each verse to the appropriate picture. Let younger children refer to the easel.

Learning objective
To act out a familiar rhyme. (Creative Development)

Group size
Up to four children.

POOR JACK!

(Rhyme – 'Jack and Jill'.) Copy the photocopiable sheet for each child. Explain that Jack had other accidents besides falling down the hill. Say that at different times, he hurt his eye, broke his arm and cut his knee. How might these accidents have happened? Ask the children to stick on collage materials (including small pieces of bandage and plasters) to make an eyepatch, a sling and a plaster. Let younger children draw them. Ask older children to write a sentence under their picture to explain what happened.

Learning objective
To think about how to help a poorly person. (Personal, Social and Emotional Development)

Group size
Up to six children.

PAGE 63
HOW MANY FLOWERS?

(Rhyme – 'Mary, Mary, Quite Contrary'.) Copy the photocopiable sheet for each child. Tell the children that when Mary planted her seeds, she made a sign at the end of each row showing what kind of seeds they were. Ask the children to count the flowers in each row, and to write the numbers on the matching signs. Help younger children to point to each flower as they count. Write the numbers faintly for them to trace over. Ask older children to cut out the rows of flowers and put them in order from most to fewest.

Learning objective
To count groups of flowers and write the matching numbers. (Mathematical Development)

Group size
Up to five children.

PAGE 61
DOES IT RHYME?

(Rhyme – 'Jack and Jill'.) Make a copy of the photocopiable sheet for each child plus one A3-size copy. Display the large copy on an easel. Read through the rhyme with the children, asking them to clap on the second word of each rhyming pair (such as 'hill', 'crown' and so on). Read the rhyme again, this time circling each pair of rhyming words in a separate colour. Remove the display sheet. Give each child five different coloured crayons and ask them to circle each pair of rhyming words in a separate colour. Let younger children refer to the display sheet. Make sheets of other well-known rhymes for older children and ask them to circle the pairs of rhyming words.

Learning objective
To recognize pairs of rhyming words. (Language and Literacy)

Group size
Up to six children.

PAGE 64
WHAT COLOUR?

(Rhyme – 'Mary, Mary, Quite Contrary'.) Copy the photocopiable sheet for each child and make one A3-size copy. Show the children the large copy and talk about the different flowers. Encourage the children to look through flower books to find out the colours of the flowers. Provide each child with their own photocopiable sheet and let them colour the flowers according to their own discoveries and preferences such as red tulips, pink carnations and so on. Let younger children use damp cotton buds dipped in a little dry powder paint to colour their flowers. Ask older children to find out about and paint some other flowers.

Learning objective
To observe and learn about the colours of different flowers. (Knowledge and Understanding of the World)

Group size
Up to six children.

PAGE 62
WHICH WAY?

(Rhyme – 'Jack and Jill'.) Make a copy of the photocopiable sheet for each child. Ask them to draw Jack and Jill's routes from their house, up and down the hill and back home. Let younger children have plenty of practice in tracing the route with their fingers or play people first. Encourage older children to use the words 'left' and 'right' to describe the route. Ensure that the children turn the sheet upside-down as they go down the hill to simulate the direction that Jack and Jill would be facing.

Learning objective
To develop pencil control and co-ordination. (Physical Development)

Group size
Up to five children.

PAGE 65
MOVING MARY

(Rhyme – 'Mary, Mary, Quite Contrary'.) Mount a copy of the photocopiable sheet onto card for each child. Help each child to cut along the marked lines on each side of the flowering bush to make a slot. Then ask them to cut along the top of the flowers on the lines indicated. Now cut out Mary and the attached strip. Let the children colour the flowers and Mary before threading the strip underneath the bush so that Mary is visible behind it. Let the children slowly pull the strip to make Mary appear to be moving.

Learning objective
To create a moving picture. (Knowledge and Understanding of the World)

Group size
Up to four children.

PAGE 66
GET WELL, HUMPTY!

Learning objective
To make a card for Humpty. (Personal, Social and Emotional Development)

Group size
Up to five children.

(Rhyme – 'Humpty Dumpty'.) Mount a copy of the photocopiable sheet onto card for each child. Explain how a get well card should have a picture of something to cheer up the poorly person. What do they think Humpty would like to look at? Ask each child to draw a picture of this on their sheet. Now help them to cut out the get well card and attach it to a piece of blank card with adhesive tape. Ask each child to write, 'Love from...' inside. Ask younger children to draw and colour balloons for Humpty's 'I am better!' party. Encourage older children to write their own message.

PAGE 67
WHAT HAPPENED NEXT?

Learning objective
To think about further endings for the rhyme. (Language and Literacy)

Group size
Up to four children.

(Rhyme – 'Humpty Dumpty'.) Make a copy of the photocopiable sheet for each child. Ask the children to think about what might have happened to Humpty Dumpty after the King's horses and men decided that they could not make him better. Perhaps the King's men brought a cart to take him to hospital or telephoned for an ambulance. Ask each child to cut out their chosen 'ending' from the three pictures, and to stick it in the blank space. Cut out all three pictures for younger children to choose from. Ask older children to think of a fourth possible outcome, and to draw it in the blank space.

PAGE 68
MEND HUMPTY

Learning objective
To assemble a jigsaw puzzle. (Physical Development)

Group size
Up to four children.

(Rhyme – 'Humpty Dumpty'.) Mount a copy of the photocopiable sheet onto card for each child. Draw four random lines right across the picture and ask the children to cut carefully along the lines to create five separate pieces of card. Can they put Humpty together again? Make a four-piece jigsaw by ruling and cutting out three lines for younger children. Challenge older children to make a seven- or eight-piece jigsaw puzzle.

PAGE 69
THEY CAN TALK!

Learning objective
To match dialogue with characters. (Language and Literacy)

Group size
Up to five children.

(Rhyme – 'Hey Diddle, Diddle!'.) Make a copy of the photocopiable sheet for each child, plus one A3-size copy. Display the large copy on an easel. Sing the song, 'Hey Diddle, Diddle!' with the children. Ask them what they think each of the characters might have been saying. For example, 'What do you think the cow said just before she jumped over the moon?'. Read the speech bubbles and match them to the characters with a line. Now let the children try on their own sheets. Let younger children refer to the display sheet. Suggest that older children cut out the characters, stick them onto card and make them into cylinders for finger puppets. They could use the speech bubble dialogue for their puppets.

PAGE 70
HIDE-AND-SEEK

Learning objective
To use positional language. (Mathematical Development)

Group size
Up to four children.

(Rhyme – 'Hey Diddle, Diddle!'.) Make a copy of the photocopiable sheet for each child and one A3-sized copy. Cut out the words from the bottom of the large sheet. Display the large sheet and talk about the positions of the characters in the picture. Read the sentences and ask the children to help you use Blu-Tack to stick the words in the right gaps. Remove the display sheet. Give each child a photocopiable sheet, ask them to cut out the words and stick them in the gaps. Cut out the words for younger children and write the words in the gaps. Ask them to match the words before gluing them on top. Let older children write the words in the gaps.

PAGE 71
PUPPET SHOW!

Learning objective
To use puppets to tell a story. (Creative Development)

Group size
Up to four children.

(Rhyme – 'Hey Diddle, Diddle!'.) Mount the photocopiable sheet onto card for each child. Ask them to colour and cut out the characters. Show the children how to stick a lollipop stick at the bottom of each character with sticky tape. Ask each child in turn to tell the rhyme, using the puppets

appropriately. Alternatively, let two children share the puppets and perform a 'play'. Let younger children colour the characters with a damp cotton bud dipped in a little dry powder paint. Cut out the characters for them, and attach the sticks. Ask older children to create stick puppets based on other songs and rhymes such as 'Old MacDonald Had a Farm'.

PAGE 72
MOUSE TIME

Learning objective
To identify four different times on a clock face. (Mathematical Development)

Group size
Up to four children.

(Rhyme – 'Hickory, Dickory, Dock'.) Make a copy of the photocopiable sheet for each child and one A3-size display copy. Give each child a card clock. Talk about the pictures that show daily activities in the life of the 'Hickory Mouse'. What time do they think the activities are happening? Ask the children to make these times on their card clocks and to draw the hands on the clocks on the sheet to match. With younger children, draw the hands for them and ask them to move the hands on their card clocks to match. Encourage older children to cut out a clock-face from the sheet and stick it on a small box painted brown to make a 'grandfather clock'. Stick on two cotton buds as the pendulums.

PAGE 73
UP THE CLOCK

(Rhyme – 'Hickory, Dickory, Dock'.) Copy the photocopiable sheet onto thin card for each child. Ask them to colour the clock and the mouse, cut out the mouse, and cut along the solid, marked lines. Ask each child to place the blank part of the sheet underneath the clock picture, and to stick adhesive tape down the left-hand side to make a stand-up card. Help each child to punch a hole in the centre of the clock-face, stick a piece of string onto the mouse and to thread the string through the hole, securing it to the blank part of the card with adhesive tape. When the card is opened, the mouse will appear to climb up the clock. Invite older children to write the rhyme inside the card. (See 'Climbing Jack' on page 39, for a similar activity.)

Learning objective
To make a moving model. (Knowledge and Understanding of the World)

Group size
Four children.

PAGE 74
TIME MIMES

(Rhyme – 'Hickory, Dickory, Dock'.) Copy the photocopiable sheet for each child and make one A3-size copy. Display the large copy and ask the children to mime the actions and to say at what time of the day each action is likely to occur. Set the time on a demonstration clock and point to the matching clock-face on the display sheet. With the children's help, draw lines from each 'action' to an appropriate 'time'. Let the children repeat the activity on their own copy of the sheet. Suggest that older children design a similar sheet showing their activities at the weekend.

Learning objective
To mime actions corresponding to certain times of the day. (Physical Development)

Group size
Up to six children.

Happy pets

◆ Cut out the animals and stick them next to the correct pictures.

A full cupboard

◆ Cut and fold to make a cupboard for Mother Hubbard. Fill it with food.

_____ cut

------------ fold

Your turn!

◆ Draw a line from each verse to the correct picture.

Old Mother Hubbard
Went to the cupboard,
To fetch her poor dog a bone;
But when she got there,
The cupboard was bare
And so the poor dog had none!

She went to the barber's
To buy him a wig;
But when she came back,
He was dancing a jig!

The dame made a curtsey,
The dog made a bow;
The dame said, 'Your servant',
The dog, said 'Bow-wow!'

Poor Jack!

◆ Please give Jack an eyepatch, a sling for his arm and a plaster for his knee.

Does it rhyme?

◆ Circle each pair of rhyming words in a different colour.

Jack and Jill

Went up the hill

To fetch a pail of water;

Jack fell down

And broke his crown

And Jill came tumbling after.

Then up Jack got

And home did trot

As fast as he could caper;

He went to bed

To mend his head

With vinegar and brown paper.

Which way?

◆ Trace the route with a pencil.

How many flowers?

◆ Count the flowers and write the numbers on the seed packets.

What colour?

◆ Find out what colours these flowers can be and paint them.

Daffodil

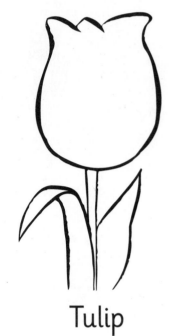

Tulip

Carnation

Lily

Moving Mary

◆ Make Mary water her flowers.

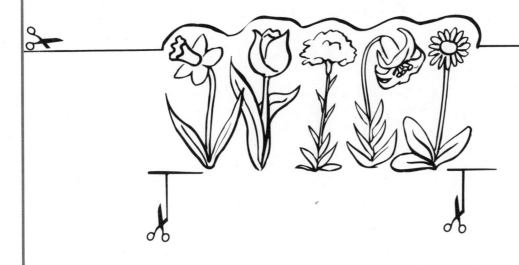

Get well, Humpty!

◆ Make a card for Humpty.

Get well soon, Humpty!

What happened next?

◆ Choose a picture for the ending. Stick it in the space.

1

2

3

4

Mend Humpty

◆ Make a jigsaw puzzle.

They can talk!

◆ Match the speech bubbles to the characters.

I am going to jump over you!

Where are we going, Dish?

What tune shall I play?

What fun this is!

Hide-and-seek

◆ Cut out the words and stick them in the correct spaces.

The dog is [   ] the log.

The cat is [   ] to the bush.

The cow is [   ] the moon.

The moon is [   ] the cow.

The dish is in [   ] of the spoon.

The spoon is [   ] the dish.

✂

over	next	in
front	under	behind

Puppet show!

◆ Colour, cut out and make lollipop stick puppets.

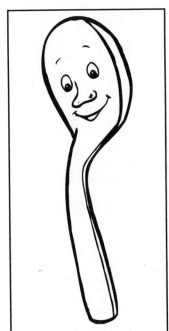

Mouse time

◆ Draw hands on the clocks to show the times in the pictures.

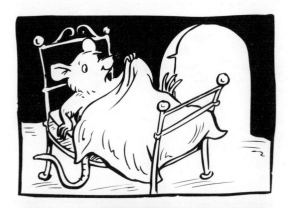 

Up the clock

◆ Make the mouse run up the clock.

Time mimes

◆ Draw lines to match the activities and the correct times.

ACTION AND COUNTING RHYMES

PAGE 79
LOOK AFTER IT!

Learning objective
To talk about looking after growing things. (Personal, Social and Emotional Development)

Group size
Up to five children.

(Rhyme – 'Here We Go Round the Mulberry Bush'.) Make a copy of the photocopiable sheet for each child. Remind the children of the 'cold and frosty' weather in the rhyme. Would cold and frosty weather be good for growing things? Explain how seeds need light and water to grow into plants. Help each child to place some cress seeds on moist cotton wool in a disposable cup and to draw and colour what the seeds look like on their sheets. Place the cups in a sunny place. Encourage the children to keep the seeds moist and to draw pictures of them on the third and fifth days. Ask older children to incorporate their pictures into a mini book. Encourage them to add some more pages.

PAGE 80
ALPHABET FRUIT

Learning objective
To develop recognition of initial letter sounds. (Language and Literacy)

Group size
Up to four children.

(Rhyme – 'Here We Go Round the Mulberry Bush'.) Copy the photocopiable sheet for each child. Cut up small pieces of apples, pears, oranges, strawberries, raspberries and gooseberries, and put them on a plate. As each child tastes a piece of fruit, they must identify it, say its initial sound and write it in the box next to the matching picture. Ask younger children to draw a line between the trees and their letters. For older children, cut off the letters at the bottom of the sheet beforehand.

PAGE 81
ALL ACTION

Learning objective
To develop miming skills. (Physical Development)

Group size
Four children.

(Rhyme – 'Here We Go Round the Mulberry Bush'.) Make four copies of the photocopiable sheet and one A3-size copy for display. Cut out the pictures from the large copy and stick them in the right places. Adapt the words from the rhyme to match the words on the sheet and encourage the children to make the actions as you point to the pictures. Give each child a photocopiable sheet and ask them to draw the right stick person in each space. Cut out the pictures for younger children and ask them to glue them on their sheet. Ask older children to work in pairs and each draw an animal for their partner to mime.

PAGE 82
THANK YOU, DOCTOR!

Learning objective
To write a 'thank-you' note. (Personal, Social and Emotional Development)

Group size
Up to five children.

(Rhyme – 'Miss Polly Had a Dolly'.) Copy the photocopiable sheet for each child. Talk about how people say 'thank you' to doctors for helping them to get better. Ask each child to write a note saying, 'Thank you for looking after me, love from...' using emergent writing, overwriting or copying. Ask each child to cut out and stick the envelope and write their doctor's name on it (use

children's records or ask parents for this information). Suggest that each child give their note to their doctor on their next visit. Scribe the words for younger children and encourage them to try to sign their own names. Suggest that older children write their doctors' addresses on the envelopes.

PAGE 83
PRESCRIPTION TIME

(Rhyme – 'Miss Polly Had a Dolly'.) Make a copy of the photocopiable sheet for each child. Explain how doctors write 'prescriptions' – notes to tell the chemist what medicine to give a patient. Remind them of the rhyme and set up the role-play area as a doctor's surgery. Provide copies of the prescription sheet for the children to use in their play. Let each child have a turn to be the doctor, and encourage them to write the prescription using emergent writing, overwriting or copying. Scribe the words for younger children and encourage older children to include as much detail as possible.

PAGE 84
MY TELEPHONE BOOK

(Rhyme – 'Miss Polly Had a Dolly'.) Copy the photocopiable sheet for each child and ask them to cut out the page shapes and staple them together. Invite the children to write their first names on the cover. Ask them to tell you the names of four people to include in their book. Help them to write the first letter of each person's name on the 'tabs' and ask them to draw each person's face in the rectangles. Let them take their books home to ask for help to write in the numbers. Cut and staple the books

for younger children and help if necessary to write their names. Challenge older children to make one or two extra pages for their books.

PAGE 85
PLANT THE SEEDS

(Rhyme – 'When All the Cows Were Sleeping'.) Make a copy of the photocopiable sheet for each child. Ask them to fold their sheet along the dotted lines and then to use a two-holed punch to make holes along both sides of the two folds. Ask each child to stick their sheet on top of a plain base sheet and 'plant' a 'seed' in each hole by filling it in with a felt-tipped pen. Make the holes for younger children to fill. Suggest that older children count the holes, and as they fill them in, ask how many more seeds will be needed to complete the row.

PAGE 86
MEND THE SCARECROW

(Rhyme – 'When All the Cows Were Sleeping'.) Make a copy of the photocopiable sheet for each child. Explain that one windy night, half of the scarecrow was blown away. Discuss with the children what is missing in the picture and ask each child if they will help the farmer by drawing the missing parts of the scarecrow. Help younger children by lightly drawing the missing side for them to draw over. Ask older children, in pairs, to draw a lapel, buttons, a top and bottom pocket on one half of the scarecrow's jacket and a patterned trouser leg. Suggest that each child gives their sheet to their partner to complete the picture.

PAGE 87

A DINGLE-DANGLE SCARECROW

Learning objective
To decorate a scarecrow. (Creative Development)

Group size
Up to four children.

(Rhyme – 'When All the Cows Were Sleeping'.) Copy the photocopiable sheet for each child and ask them to decorate the body parts by sticking on collage materials. Ask each child to cut out the parts and stick them to a kitchen roll tube. Help the children to make their scarecrows stand by making slits round the bottom of the tube, splaying them out and securing them to a piece of card with sticky tape. Let younger children simply decorate the scarecrow. Invite older children to decorate large rectangles of paper to represent fields of crops. Cover a table with the fields to make a 'farm' with a scarecrow in each 'field'.

PAGE 88

CURRANT BUN LOTTO

Learning objective
To match dots (currants) to numbers. (Mathematical Development)

Group size
Up to seven children.

(Rhyme – 'Five Currant Buns'.) Copy the photocopiable sheet for each child. Write the numbers 1 to 5 on separate pieces of blank A4 paper. Give each child a sheet and fifteen currants. Hold up each number and ask the children to put the same number of currants on the matching bun, and to write the number in the box. When all the buns have been matched, let the children eat the currants. Ask younger children to draw lines from the buns to the numbers at the bottom of the sheet. Ask older children questions such as, 'If the boy in the shop ate two buns – one with two currants, and the other with three currants – how many currants did he eat altogether?'.

PAGE 89

WHAT NEXT?

(Rhyme – 'Five Currant Buns'.) Copy the photocopiable sheet for each child. Make one A3-size copy for display. Collect the utensils and ingredients and ensure that the children wash their hands. As the children make the buns, read the display sheet several times with them. When the buns have been made, give out the sheets and ask the children to cut along the marked lines. Collect the column of picture 'clues' from each child and ask them to mix up the sentences and then put them back in the correct order, using the numbers to help them. Give them the picture clues to match to the sentences and encourage them to re-read the sentences using shared reading. Let younger children use the picture clues to put the sentences in order. Challenge older children to put the sentences in order without the help of the pictures or numbers.

Learning objective
To follow a currant bun recipe. (Knowledge and Understanding of the World)

Group size
Four children.

PAGE 90

PLAYING SHOP

(Rhyme – 'Five Currant Buns'.) Copy the photocopiable sheet for each child. Choose one of the children to be the 'shopkeeper' and say the rhyme together. Let the children take turns to buy a bun from the 'shopkeeper' as they say the rhyme. Now give each child their sheet and ask them to cut out the buns and to make the boy into a stick puppet by cutting him out and sticking him to a lolly stick. Repeat the rhyme and let each child move their puppet towards the buns and remove one at the appropriate points of the rhyme.

Learning objective
To act out a familiar rhyme. (Creative Development)

Group size
Six children.

PAGE 91

MY DREAM

(Rhyme – 'There Were Ten in the Bed'.) Make a copy of the photocopiable sheet for each child. In a cirlce, encourage the children to take turns to describe one of their dreams. Ask the children to draw their dream on the sheet giving the face a smile for a happy dream and a sad expression for a nightmare.

Learning objective
To talk about dreams. (Personal, Social and Emotional Development)

Group size
Up to six children.

PAGE 92
ROLL OVER!

Learning objective
To understand the concept of 'one less'. (Mathematical Development)

Group size
Up to four children.

(Rhyme – 'There Were Ten in the Bed'.) Provide each child with a copy of the photocopiable sheet together with ten wide straws. Invite the children to cut out the ten faces and stick them to the straws with sticky tape. Ask each child to line up their puppets side-by-side on top of a thick book (the 'bed'). As the children say the rhyme, ask them to roll their puppets off the bed at the appropriate points. Reduce the number of puppets to five for younger children. Ask older children questions such as, 'If two fell out of the bed, how many would be left?'.

PAGE 93
A PRETTY QUILT

Learning objective
To decorate a 'quilt' cover using felt-tipped pen patterns. (Creative Development)

Group size
Up to five children.

(Rhyme – 'There Were Ten in the Bed'.) Make a copy of the photocopiable sheet for each child. Explain that each person in the bed has started a pattern on the quilt and they need help to finish it. Ask each child to choose ten different coloured felt-tipped pens (one colour per panel) to complete the patterns. Finish the patterns for younger children and let them trace over them. Help older children to use a large needle and thread (under supervision) to make running stitches around the outer edge of the 'quilt'.

PAGE 94
FIND THE RHYMES

Learning objective
To match rhyming pairs. (Language and Literacy)

Group size
Up to six children.

(Rhyme – 'One, Two, Buckle My Shoe'.) Make a copy of the photocopiable sheet for each child plus one A3-size copy. Chant the rhyme with the children, pausing before each rhyming word. Display the large copy and 'read' the pictures on the left and point to the rhyming numbers. Similarly, 'read' the pictures on the right and point to the rhyming words. Ask the children to make up an alternative rhyme using the pictures to help them, such as: 'One, two – let's use the glue' and so on. Ask each child to join both columns of words with the rhyming numbers. Let younger children match the words on the left only. Challenge older children to write the odd numbers with matching pictures on a separate piece of paper.

PAGE 95
LAY THEM STRAIGHT

Learning objective
To appreciate conservation of number. (Mathematical Development)

Group size
Up to four children.

(Rhyme – 'One, Two, Buckle My Shoe'.) Copy the photocopiable sheet for each child. Give each child eight sticks (or straws) the same length as the sticks on the sheet. Ask the children to match their sticks on top of the drawings and to write the numbers in the boxes. Use the opportunity to check the children's understanding of conservation of number. Make a row of sticks in front of a child. Ask them to count them. Now spread out the same row of sticks. Ask the child to tell you how many there are now. Does the child need to count them? Let younger children simply match the sticks with the drawings. Challenge older children to make four different patterns or 'pictures' with sets of five, seven and ten sticks.

PAGE 96
BY NUMBERS

Learning objective
To relate numbers of the rhyme to actions. (Physical Development)

Group size
Up to five children.

(Rhyme – 'One, Two, Buckle My Shoe'.) Give a copy of the photocopiable sheet to each child. Write the numbers two, four, six, eight and ten on separate sheets of A4 paper. Chant the rhyme, holding up the numbers, and ask the children to point to the pictures on their sheet and mime the actions. Now ask each child to cut out the numbers and stick them in the right spaces. Let younger children match the pictures and numbers with a line. With older children, chant the following:
Zero, one – wave to John
Two, three – climb a tree
Four, five – creep up to a hive
Six, seven – swim in Devon
Eight, nine – draw a line.
   Hold up the numbers 1, 3, 5, 7 and 9 and ask the children to mime the actions to match the numbers.

Look after it!

◆ Draw what your cress seeds look like as they grow.

1st day

3rd day

5th day

Alphabet fruit

◆ Write the first letters of each of the fruits in the boxes.

o   a   p   g   r   s

All action

◆ Draw the correct person in each space.
This is the way we...

stretch our arms	put our hands in the air
sit down on the floor	lie down on the floor

  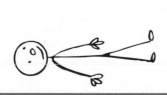 

Thank you, doctor!

◆ Cut out, fold and stick to make an envelope.

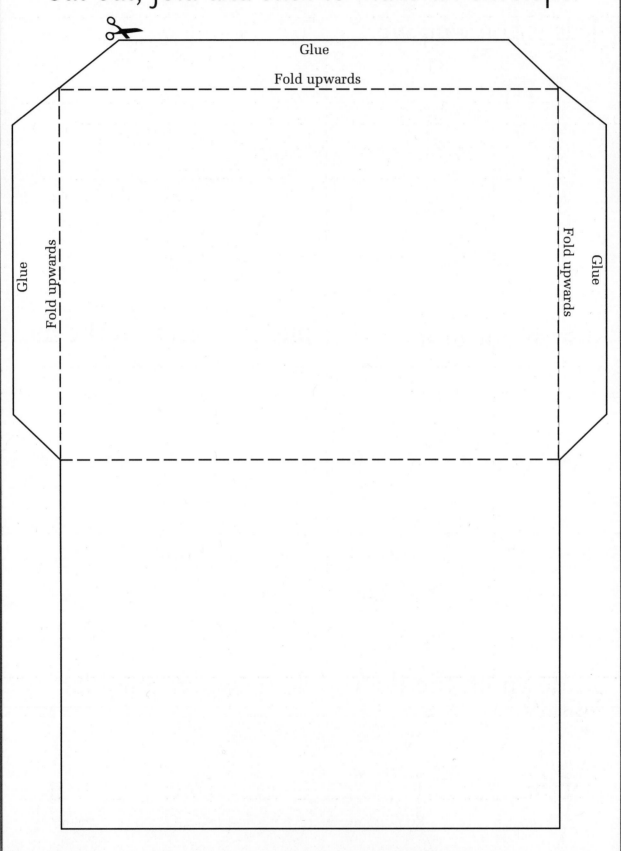

Prescription time

◆ Write a doctor's prescription.

Name	Age
_____	_____

Dose	Name of medication

Signed

Doctor_____   Date _____

My telephone book

◆ Make your own telephone book.

This telephone book
belongs to

_____

_____

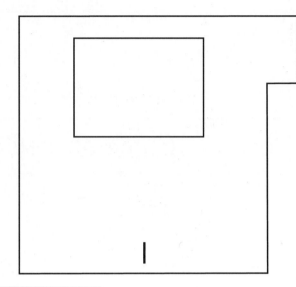

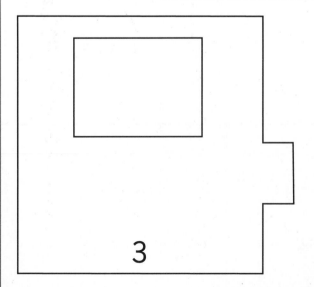

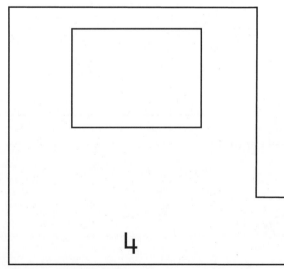

Plant the seeds

◆ Make the holes and put one seed into each hole.

Mend the scarecrow

◆ Draw the other half of the scarecrow.

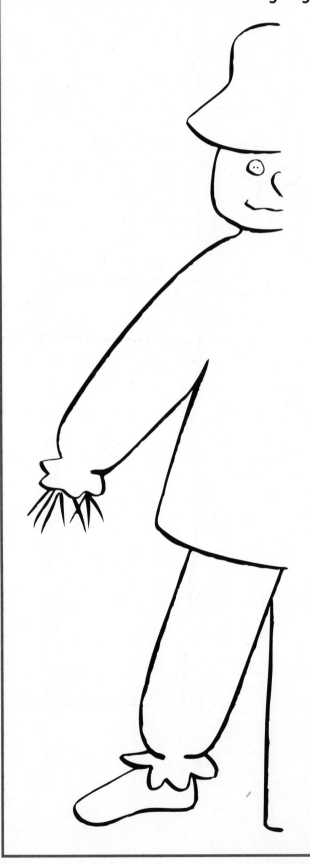

A dingle-dangle scarecrow

◆ Decorate, cut out and stick to a tube.

Currant bun lotto

◆ Write the number of currants on each bun.

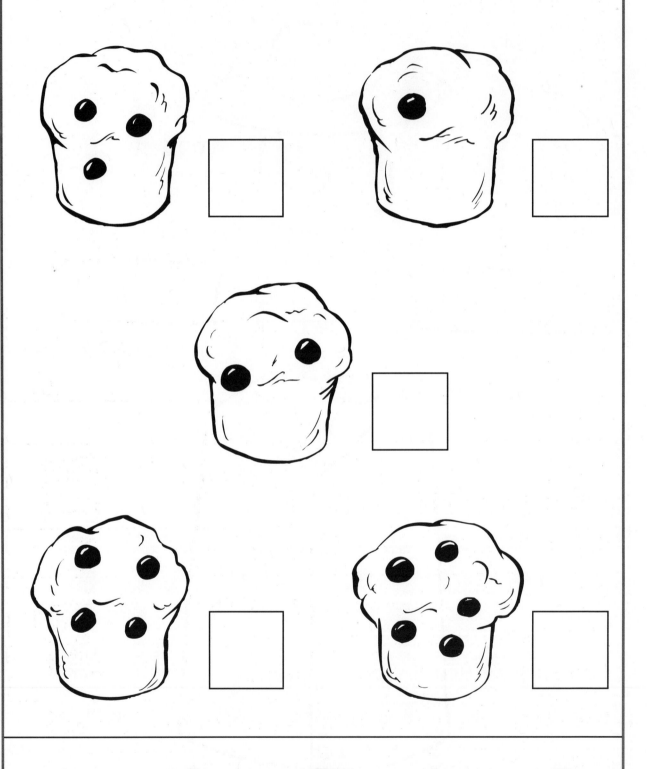

| 1 | 2 | 3 | 4 | 5 |

What next?

◆ Cut out the sentences and put them in the correct order.

<u>Ingredients</u>

150g castor sugar

2 eggs

125g soft margarine

175g self-raising flour

2 teaspoons currants

<u>Utensils</u>

1 mixing bowl

1 wooden spoon

Patty tins

Cooling tray

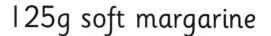

What to do

1 Ask a grown-up to heat the oven to gas mark 6, 200°C, 400°F.

2 Put 18 paper cases in patty tins.

3 Put all the ingredients in a bowl. Mix them together for two or three minutes with a wooden spoon.

4 Half-fill the cases with the mixture.

5 Bake the buns for 15 minutes. Then let them cool on a wire tray.

Playing shop

◆ Make the boy into a stick puppet. Cut out the buns and let him buy them.

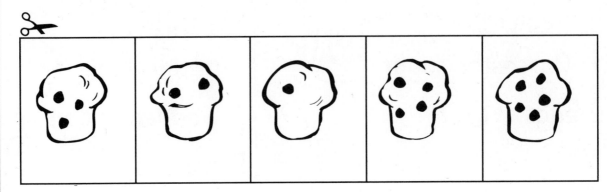

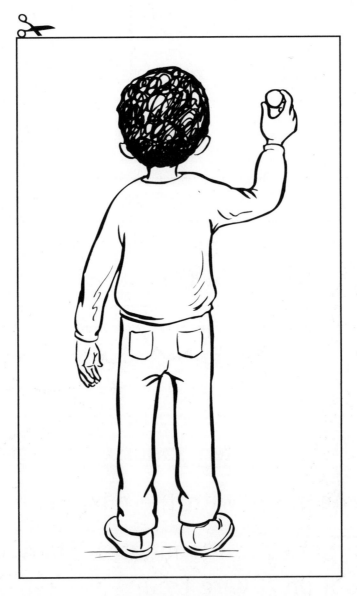

My dream

◆ Draw your dream in the bubble. Make your face happy or sad.

Roll over!

◆ Cut along the lines. Stick the faces onto straws to make puppets.

A pretty quilt

◆ Finish the patterns on the quilt.

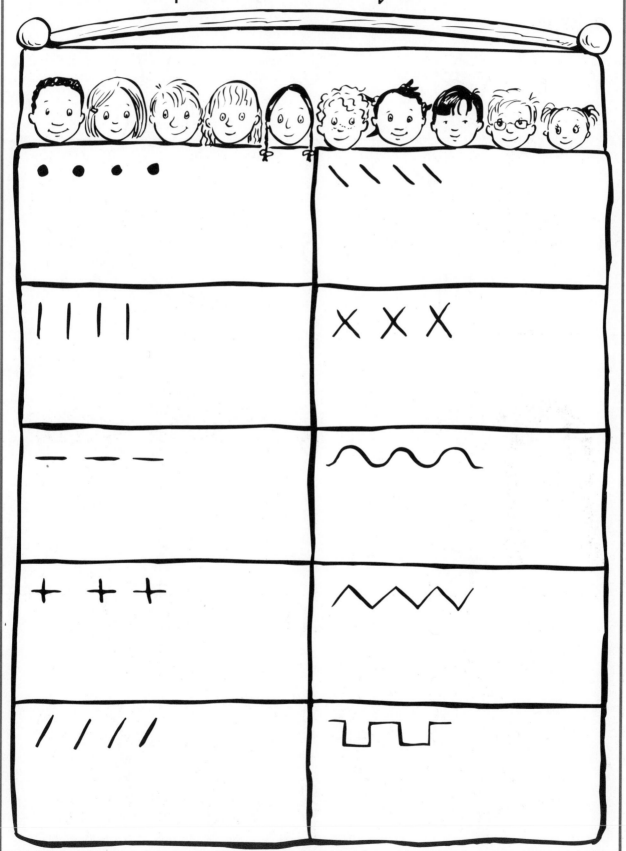

Find the rhymes

◆ Match the pictures and rhyming numbers with a line.

4

2

6

10

8

Lay them straight

◆ Place the sticks on top and write the matching numbers in the boxes.

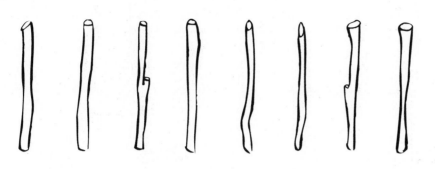

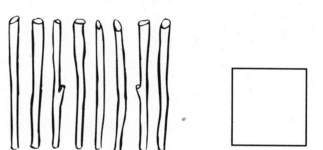

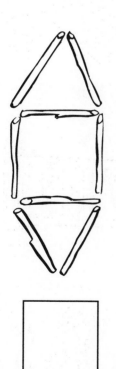

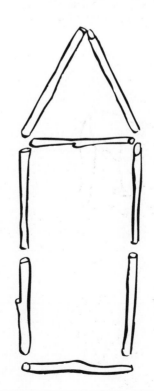

By numbers

◆ Cut out the numbers and stick them next to their rhyming pictures.

| 2 | 4 | 6 | 8 | 10 |